动脑想一想

Social Emotional and Multicultural Learning |
Non-Fiction Series

Copyright 2022 by Level Learning, INC. and Washington Yu Ying PCS™
Original and Edited Text Copyright © 2022 by Washington Yu Ying PCS™

All rights reserved. No part of this book in whole or part may be reproduced without written permission from the publisher.

Published by Level Learning, INC.

Content Contributors:
Washington Yu Ying PCS™
Level Learning - Ya-Ching Chang

Illustrations by: Josh Taira

Leveling classification based on Level Learning standard. For full description, visit www.levellearning.com

ISBN 978-1-64040-074-0
Simplified Chinese Edition

Level Learning:
Level Learning provides a literacy focused curriculum specifically designed for K-12 Chinese as a Second Language classrooms. Our program offers 20 levels of specific and detailed objectives, leveled texts and passages, mastery-based online assessment, and analytics to enable data-driven instruction. Level Learning reading curriculum for both literature and informational text emphasize grammar and comprehension skills to help teachers develop confident and independent Chinese language readers. The non-fiction series of books are specifically designed to support our informational text course based on multiple national standards. To learn more about our entire offering, visit www.levellearning.com.

About Washington Yu Ying PCS™:
Washington Yu Ying PCS is a Mandarin English dual language immersion International Baccalaureate (IB) World school. Yu Ying's mission is to inspire and prepare young people to create a better world by challenging them to reach their full potential in a nurturing Chinese/English educational environment. Yu Ying's comprehensive IB, dual immersion curriculum equips students with global competencies for success in the real world. As a leader in immersion education, Yu Ying is determined to advance Chinese language programs and global citizenry education by helping other schools create and strengthen their Chinese programs. For more information, email: products@washingtonyuying.org

今天的作业太难,怎么办?动脑想一想。

我可以看笔记和课本。

我也可以问同学。

每天**忘记**带东西,怎么办?动脑想一想。

我可以写在记事本上。

我也可以记在月历上。

考试考不好，怎么办？动脑想一想。

我可以多练习几次。我也可以问老师。

碰到了难题,怎么办?
动脑想一想。

我不用别人告诉我。我要学会自己找答案。

动脑想一想。每个问题都会有答案。

动脑想一想。所有的事情都会变简单。

Glossary

	Pinyin	English Definition
作业	zuò yè	homework
太难	tài nán	too hard
怎么办	zěn me bàn	what to do
动脑	dòng nǎo	to think/to use your brain
想一想	xiǎng yì xiǎng	to think about it
笔记	bǐ jì	notes
课本	kè běn	textbook
问	wèn	to ask
忘记	wàng jì	to forget
记事本	jì shì běn	notebook
月历	yuè lì	calendar
考试	kǎo shì	exam
练习	liàn xí	to practice
几次	jǐ cì	several times

	Pinyin	English Definition
碰	pèng	to meet/to encounter
难题	nán tí	difficult question
找	zhǎo	to find
答案	dá àn	answer
变	biàn	to change
简单	jiǎn dān	simple